Contents

KT-116-378

Words appearing in the text in bold,
like this, are explained in the Glossary.

 Find out more about how things are
made at www.heinemannexplore.co.uk

What is in a book?

Some books tell stories. Other books give you information about something. Both kinds of books may contain pictures as well as words.

How Is a BOOK Made?

Angela Royston

Heinemann LIBRARY

Young Explorer

www.heinemann.co.uk/library

Visit our website to find out more information about Heinemann Library books.

To order:

☎ Phone 44 (0) 1865 888066

▤ Send a fax to 44 (0) 1865 314091

▢ Visit the Heinemann Bookshop at www.heinemann.co.uk/library to browse our catalogue and order online.

First published in Great Britain by Heinemann Library, Halley Court, Jordan Hill, Oxford OX2 8EJ, part of Harcourt Education. Heinemann is a registered trademark of Harcourt Education Ltd.

Editorial: Lucy Thunder and Louise Galpine
Design: Jo Hinton-Malivoire and AMR
Illustration: Art Construction
Picture Research: Melissa Allison and Debra Weatherley
Production: Camilla Smith

Originated by RMW
Printed and bound in China by South China Printing Company

The paper used to print this book comes from sustainable resources

ISBN 0 431 05044 9 (hardback)
09 08 07 06 05
10 9 8 7 6 5 4 3 2 1

ISBN 0 431 05051 1 (paperback)
10 09 08 07 06
10 9 8 7 6 5 4 3 2 1

British Library Cataloguing in Publication Data
Royston, Angela
How is a book made?
686

A full catalogue record for this book is available from the British Library.

Acknowledgements
The Publishers would like to thank the following for permission to reproduce photographs: Art Directors/TRIP pp.**17** (John Ellard), **16** (Peter Kaplan); Corbis pp.**13** (David Lees), **15** (Lester Lefkowitz); Corbis/Royalty free pp.**14**, **24**; Getty Images/Image Bank p.**12**; Getty Images/Image Bank p. **4** (Bruce Laurence); Getty Images p.**28** (PhotoDisc); Harcourt Education pp.**25**, **28**; Harcourt Education Ltd /Tudor Photography pp.**7**, **8**, **22**, **26**, **27**, **29**; Harcourt Education Ltd pp.**6**, **9** (Trevor Clifford); Lynx dpm Ltd pp.**19**, **20**, **21**, **23**; Robert Harding Picture Library p.**10**; Wing King Tong p.**18**.

Cover photograph of books reproduced with permission of Harcourt Education Ltd/Tudor Photography.

The Publishers would like to thank Camilla Smith for her assistance in the preparation of this book.

Key
materials for paper
materials for ink and glue

This world map shows some places that the materials for paper, ink, and glue come from.

Canada

Norway Sweden Finland Russia

NORTH AMERICA

EUROPE

ASIA

United States

Iraq

Libya

Venezuela

Saudi Arabia

Nigeria

SOUTH AMERICA

AFRICA

AUSTRALIA

N
W E
S

ANTARCTICA

A book is mainly made of paper, but ink and glue are used too. These **materials** come from different parts of the world.

Who makes books?

A **publisher** is a **company** that creates books. The publisher pays the **author**, the photographer, and all the people who work on the words and pictures.

These people are choosing the cover of a new book.

Many people work for the publisher.
Sales people sell the books when they
are finished. Other people look after the
company's money.

Creating a book

A book can have words and pictures.
The **designer** arranges the words and
pictures on each page.

The designer works
on a computer.

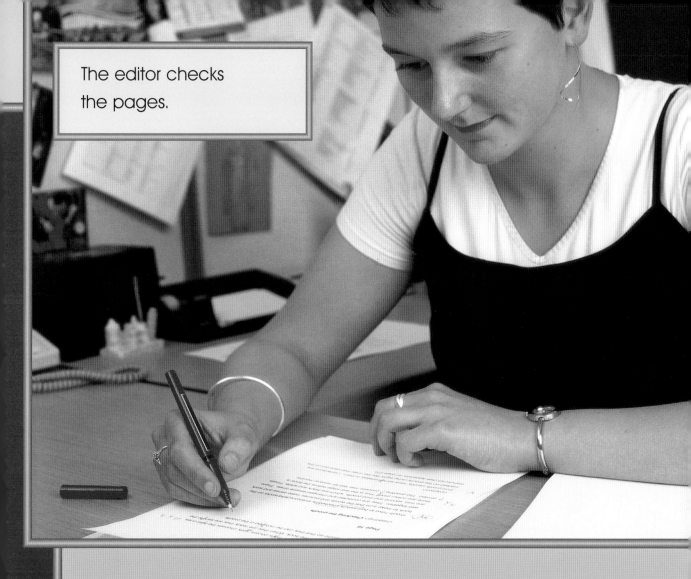

The editor checks
the pages.

When the designer has finished working
on the book he or she prints out the
pages. The **author** and the **editor**
check the pages. The book design
is then copied onto a CD.

Getting ready to print

The **publisher** sends the CD with the words and pictures to the **printers**. The printers may be close by or they may be in a different country.

The publisher buys paper from a paper mill. The mill sends the paper to the printers. The printers buy the ink and the glue.

Huge packets of paper are taken to the printers.

Where paper comes from

Paper is made from trees. Some forests of trees are specially grown. These trees can be cut down and used to make paper.

These trees will be made into paper.

In this Italian paper factory the water and wood are mixed outdoors.

Machines crush the wood and mix it with water to make a pulp. The pulp is spread into a thin layer. As it dries it forms a sheet of paper.

Making glue

Glue is made from plastic, which comes from **oil**. The oil is found deep below the ground and under the seabed. An oil well drills into the ground to reach the oil.

The oil is taken to an oil **refinery**. There the oil is separated into petrol and other liquids. Some of the liquids are mixed with **chemicals** to make glue.

Making ink

Books with coloured pictures use four different colours of ink. Ink is made from **oil**. Different **chemicals** are added to the ink to make different colours.

People in the ink factory mix the chemicals together to get exactly the right colours. The ink is then packed and sent to the **printers**.

The printing machine

Now the **printers** are ready to print the book. First they make **metal plates**. The plates have the words and pictures from the CD put onto them.

The machine prints pages of the book on to each sheet of paper. First one side of the paper is printed, and then the other side is printed.

Several book pages fit onto one sheet of paper.

Printing colours

The machine prints each colour of ink separately. As a sheet of paper passes through the printing machine, the yellow ink prints, then the blue ink, then the red ink.

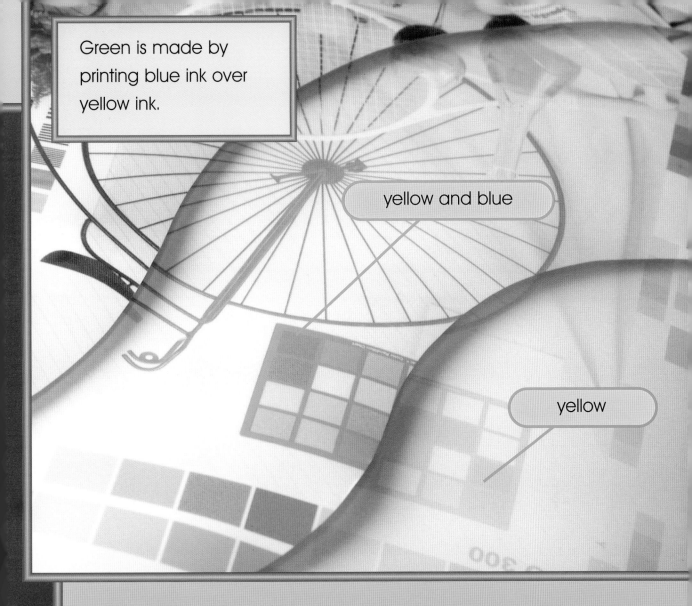

Green is made by printing blue ink over yellow ink.

yellow and blue

yellow

The last colour to print is black. With red, yellow, and blue, the four colours make all the other colours. The words are usually printed with black ink only.

Adding the cover

The cover of the book is printed separately. The cover of a hardback book is made of thick cardboard. The cover of a paperback is made of thin cardboard.

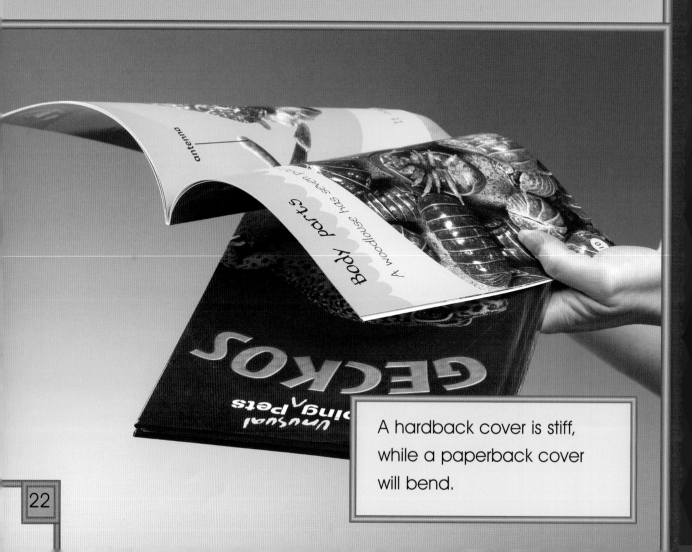

A hardback cover is stiff, while a paperback cover will bend.

A special machine folds the pages of the book and trims the three outside edges. Before the cover is glued on, the pages may be sewn together at the **spine**.

A machine adds the covers to each book.

Storing the books

Now the books are finished! The **printers** pack thousands of copies of the book into boxes. They are sent by lorry or ship to the **publisher**.

This ship has brought books from China to your country.

The publisher stores the books in a huge **warehouse**. The publisher tells bookshops, libraries, and schools they can now order these new books.

Selling the books

Bookshops, libraries, and schools order the books from the **publisher**. Workers in the **warehouse** pack up the books before sending them.

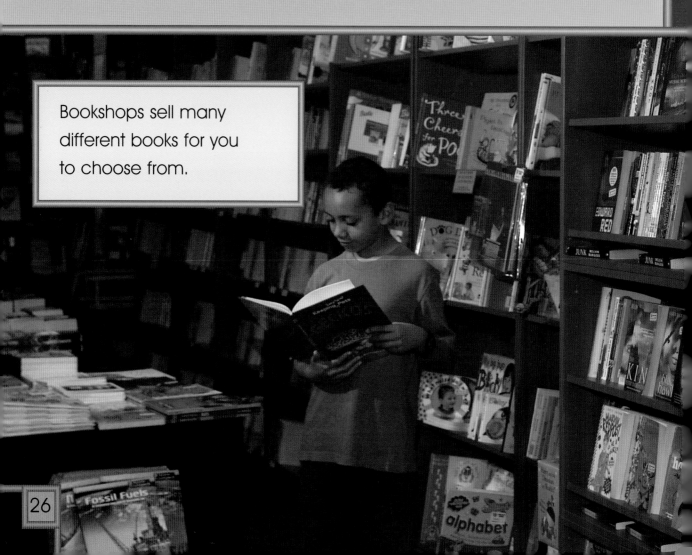

Bookshops sell many different books for you to choose from.

The bookshop keeps some of the money you pay for a book. The rest of the money goes to the publisher. The publisher uses it to create new books.

From start to finish

A book is made mostly of paper. Paper is made from trees.

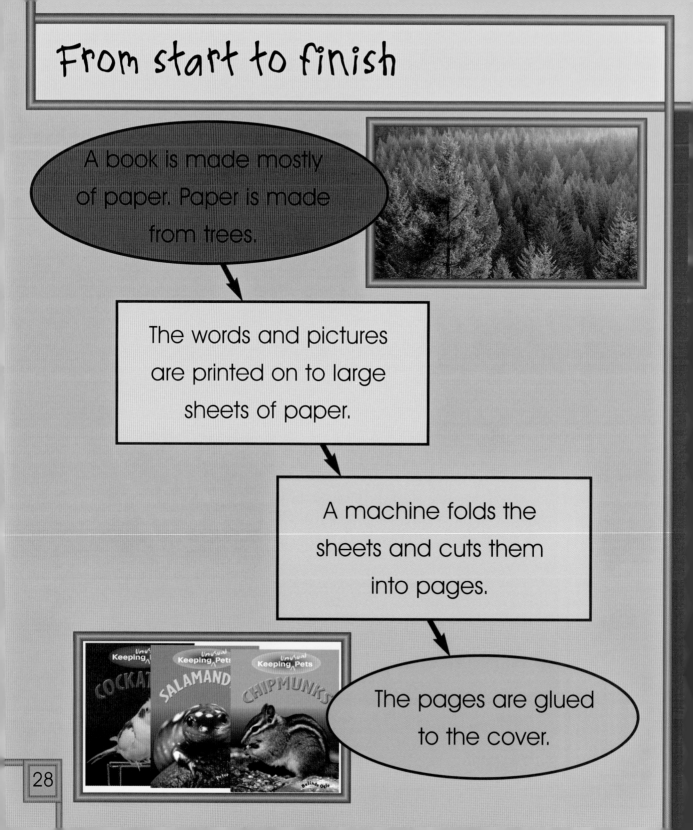

The words and pictures are printed on to large sheets of paper.

A machine folds the sheets and cuts them into pages.

The pages are glued to the cover.

A closer look

Every book tells you the names of the **publisher** and the **printer**. In many books, this information is on page 2.

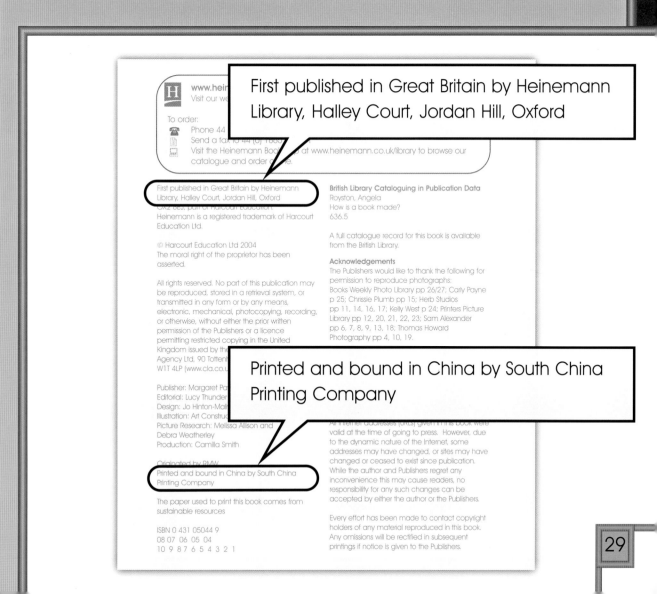

First published in Great Britain by Heinemann Library, Halley Court, Jordan Hill, Oxford

Printed and bound in China by South China Printing Company

www.hei...
Visit our we...

To order:
Phone 44...
Send a fax to 44 (0) 186...
Visit the Heinemann Boo... at www.heinemann.co.uk/library to browse our catalogue and order o...

First published in Great Britain by Heinemann Library, Halley Court, Jordan Hill, Oxford OX2 8EJ, part of Harcourt Education. Heinemann is a registered trademark of Harcourt Education Ltd.

© Harcourt Education Ltd 2004
The moral right of the proprietor has been asserted.

Publisher: Margaret Pa...
Editorial: Lucy Thunder...
Design: Jo Hinton-Mali...
Illustration: Art Constru...
Picture Research: Melissa Allison and Debra Weatherley
Production: Camilla Smith

Originated by RMW
Printed and bound in China by South China Printing Company

The paper used to print this book comes from sustainable resources

ISBN 0 431 05044 9
08 07 06 05 04
10 9 8 7 6 5 4 3 2 1

British Library Cataloguing in Publication Data
Royston, Angela
How is a book made?
636.5

A full catalogue record for this book is available from the British Library.

Acknowledgements
The Publishers would like to thank the following for permission to reproduce photographs:
Books Weekly Photo Library pp 26/27; Carly Payne p 25; Chrissie Plumb pp 15; Herb Studios pp 11, 14, 16, 17; Kelly West p 24; Printers Picture Library pp 12, 20, 21, 22, 23; Sam Alexander pp 6, 7, 8, 9, 13, 18; Thomas Howard Photography pp 4, 10, 19.

Glossary

author writer

chemical substance that things are made of

company group of people who work together

designer person who decides how something will look

editor person who is in charge of creating a new book

materials what things are made of

metal plate sheet of metal

oil liquid that forms under the ground

printers company that makes books

publisher person or company that creates new books

refinery place where oil is separated into petrol and other liquids

spine part of the cover of a book between the front cover and the back cover

warehouse building where things are stored

Places to visit

British Library, London: here you can see the first copies of classic books and learn how books were made; *www.bl.uk*

Catalyst, Widnes: hands-on and interactive exploration of how the science of chemistry affects our everyday lives; *www.catalyst.org.uk*

Eureka! The Museum for Children, Halifax: interactive exhibits exploring the world of science; *www.eureka.org.uk*

Glasgow Science Centre, Glasgow: fun way to learn more about science and technology; *www.glasgowsciencecentre.org*

Magna Science Adventure Centre, Rotherham: science as an adventurous journey; *www.visitmagna.co.uk*

The Science Museum, London: many special exhibitions as well as the museum's historic collection; *www.sciencemuseum.org*

Scienceworks, Melbourne, Australia. *www.scienceworks.museum.vic.gov.au*

Index